C000234882

THE CR

TRUTH & FICTION

An Analysis

of

the Netflix Series

THE CROWN

HUGO VICKERS

ZULEIKA

First published in 2017 by Zuleika

89 Lexham Gardens, London, W8 6JN

ISBN 978-1-9997770-5-0

Printed and bound in Great Britain by
Marston Book Services Ltd, Oxfordshire

ACKNOWLEDGMENTS

The author wishes to thank Tom Perrin and Louise Naudé at Zuleika for their judicious editing and magnificent support, Bridget Harrison at *The Times*, Jesse Norman, MP for a spontaneous idea instantly adopted, and Thibault de Bray for suggesting the title.

INTRODUCTION

The Crown is a lavish Netflix series which has now run to twenty episodes. Since I am frequently described as an expert on the Royal Family, particularly when it comes to the period that the series covers, I have been bombarded by questions as to what in Series 1 is true and what is false. And so I have decided to put my thoughts down on paper.

I do not approve of *The Crown* because it depicts real people in situations which are partly true and partly false; but unfortunately most viewers take it all as gospel truth. And whilst I accept that fiction can be used as a device to illuminate true events, I also believe that it can be used to pervert the facts and create false impressions.

Unquestionably, this has been a highly successful series, which is watched with intense interest across the globe. The settings and costumes are of high quality, the acting is good, and it all looks convincing. Peter Morgan is an intelligent writer; I much enjoyed his film *The Queen*, and the stage production of *The Audience*. The real Queen clearly inspires great performances from actresses such as Prunella Scales and Helen Mirren, and

Claire Foy also portrays her beautifully. What I failed to appreciate at the end of Series 1, but wholly accept now, was that *The Crown* did a great job in reminding a younger generation that the Queen and Prince Philip were once young themselves.

But, sadly, there are many lapses into poor taste.

I understand that each episode needs conflict and drama. One of the devices used in Series 2 is to take two simple events which did happen, and clash them against each other to create something which did not. To take an example from Episode 8: yes, the Queen and Prince Philip entertained the Kennedys at Buckingham Palace (on 5 June 1961); and yes, the Queen visited Nkrumah in Ghana (between 9 and 20 November 1961). But the Queen did not go to Ghana for the trivial reason that she wished to pull one over on Mrs Kennedy – she went there to ensure that Ghana remained part of the Commonwealth.

Much has been written about the massive budget for this series, and its attention to detail. I am afraid I found quite a number of mistakes, especially in respect of Orders and decorations. Having worked on films myself, I know how hard it is to make sure these are correct, and sometimes shortcuts have to be taken. But one must try to get the details right, and so I have pointed out some of these errors. These, however, are trivial things in comparison to the events shown as having happened, when in fact they did not.

The cruellest and most undeserved victim of the series is Prince Philip, portrayed as a fractious, bumptious Jack the Lad, very much the villain. Watching the series, I failed to find the man who, in 1962, was advancing Anglo-German relations through remarks such as, 'It may be difficult for people to see any virtue in forgiving one's enemies, but let them reflect that it is much more likely to achieve a better future than stoking the fires of hatred and suspicion.' This fictional Prince Philip is little more than a self-centred philanderer. The real Prince Philip told his biographer, Tim Heald, 'I certainly believe in the need for a "free" press, but there is a difference between freedom and licence, and between the honest pursuit of the truth and the cynical pursuit of thoughtless – even vindictive – sensationalism.'

Fiction should help us understand the truth, not pervert it.

Hugo Pichens

1–7 December 2017

SERIES ONE

Episode 1—Wolferton Splash

The series opens with King George VI spewing blood into a lavatory pan, to indicate that he is a sick man. Before the opening credits, there is a scene in which the King invests Prince Philip as Duke of Edinburgh. Prince Philip is described as a Prince of Greece and 'of' Denmark. Then the King knights him as he bestows titles on him in the wrong order, and only afterwards gives him the Order of the Garter. There is a scene in which the King uses the 'C' word. We are introduced to the Prince Philip character, smoking a cigarette on the day before the wedding and treating it all as something of a game.

This episode introduces the various themes. We see tension between the King and Prince Philip; we meet Group Captain Peter Townsend hovering amorously around Princess Margaret, and Princess Elizabeth preparing for her future role, at work with her father.

At the 1947 royal wedding, Prince Philip's mother is depicted in a nun's habit – in reality she was a civilian then and did not adopt the habit (which she wore at the Coronation) until 1948. But this allows Queen Elizabeth (the Queen Mother) to describe her disparagingly as 'the hun nun'. But then she calls her daughter 'Elizabeth' when it was always 'Lilibet'. There are scenes of Princess Elizabeth's carefree life in Malta, though her son, Prince Charles, was not in Malta at that time.

The King has to have an operation, so we see Princess Margaret waiting anxiously with Queen Mary while the King is with his doctors. There are gory scenes of the lung being removed and then wrapped up in a copy of *The Times* (a story gleaned from Hugh Trevor-Roper's letters). There is a moment where Sir John Weir, the well-known homeopathic doctor, informs the King of the gravity of his illness even after the operation. It is curious that this role was assigned to Weir. In reality he failed to give the King proper advice. He was even mistrusted by the admirable Dr Margery Blackie, the most distinguished of homeopathic doctors, who had little time for him.

In 1948 Dermot Morrah, respected *Times* writer, reported privately that the King was in danger of losing his leg: 'One special source of anxiety is his personal physician – a homeopathic quack with a fascination for women, some of whom planted him on Edward, Prince of Wales, who bequeathed him to his successor as official medical officer. Of course they've called in good men as consultants, Cassidy and Learmouth especially, but this old menace is there all the time, and it was he who let the trouble go to this length before sounding the alarm.'

It was just as bad in 1951, in which this episode is set. Weir accompanied the King to Balmoral for the summer. The worldly doctor enjoyed himself shooting with Scottish dukes. Only when the local doctor was called in was the gravity of the King's illness appreciated, resulting in him being whisked down to London to have his lung removed. Following that, those who understood such things realised that the King's life was likely to be short.

This episode depicts Churchill becoming Prime Minister again (in October 1951), and suggests that neither he nor the King are in good health. The King is forced to wear rouge (which was the case). In reality it is not certain how much the King was told about his state of health. The episode ends with Princess Elizabeth looking at the King's boxes, and in a sense facing her destiny.

Minor mistakes: Princess Elizabeth's car has the royal coat of arms on it, which is reserved for the monarch; Lady Churchill's GBE riband at the wedding is too red and too wide.

Episode 2—Hyde Park Corner

Episode 1 warned us that the King's life was in danger. Episode 2 carries him off. It starts with Princess Elizabeth arriving in Kenya on the first leg of the proposed Commonwealth tour she is undertaking on her father's behalf.

We see the royal limousine arriving at an event and the Royal Standard fluttering on the front of it, the inference here being that Princess Elizabeth has already become Queen – but no, it is the wrong Royal Standard. Princess Elizabeth's would have had a label of three white points. Soon afterwards a cocky Prince Philip mocks a Kikuyu chieftain for wearing a medal to which he is apparently not entitled (in fact a Victoria Cross, though this is not explained). This was in February 1952, and yet Prince Philip was wearing a 1953 Coronation medal. Arguably this might not have mattered, but for the fact that he was chiding someone else for wearing the wrong medal.

As they arrive at Treetops for the fateful night of 5/6 February, the Prince Philip character does a *Crocodile Dundee* feat in seeing off a bull elephant. In reality there were no elephants there that day or night.

The scenes in which Lord Salisbury is seen plotting to get rid of Churchill have not been well received by the Cecil family due to inaccuracies. He would never have elicited the help of Lord Mountbatten, for example. Anthony Eden did not go to Sandringham to ask the King to exercise his constitutional right to remove the Prime Minister from office on account of his incapacity to run the country properly, least of all in February 1952. Churchill himself is given a fictitious secretary called Venetia Scott, so that she can play a role in Episode 4.

Following the King's death, we see a gruesome scene in which Princess Margaret visits the body of her father during the embalming process. Churchill did not broadcast in the presence of the entire Cabinet, yet his actual words are as moving to listen to today as they surely were at the time. Tommy Lascelles, the Private Secretary, is invested with a most sinister role. He is given good lines, such as when he passes on the Queen Mother's offer to Townsend to become her Comptroller at Clarence House: 'I don't expect you to accept.'

Minor mistakes: it was not Lascelles who told Churchill of the King's death, it was Sir Edward Ford; Queen Mary was told by Lady Cynthia Colville, not by a footman; it is unlikely that Princess Elizabeth had just written to her father before hearing of his death; Queen Mary did not come to Sandringham to curtsey to the new Queen (that happened at Clarence House); there is nothing to suggest that Lascelles caught Princess Margaret and Townsend kissing; contemporary evidence proves that the Queen Mother did not cry hysterically when she heard of the King's death (she was far too stoical); Martin Charteris did not disappear from royal service immediately after the King's death (he became part of the team, though no longer the new Queen's actual Private Secretary). Some of these things are acceptable under the heading of dramatic licence.

Episode 3—Windsor

Back we go to 1936, seeing Princess Elizabeth and Princess Margaret playing just before their uncle, King Edward VIII, broadcasts his Abdication speech. There is no way that Queen Mary would have come into the room to see the King and try to dissuade him from broadcasting. And Mrs Simpson was not hovering in the background as he made that speech. In reality she was in Cannes. In the real Abdication speech he was announced as 'His Royal Highness Prince Edward', not as Duke of Windsor.

Presently there are many scenes involved with the aftermath of King George VI's death: the young Queen wearing black and sometimes a black veil, and Tommy Lascelles becoming ever more the dominant figure in the Palace.

Two big issues are explored to show how Prince Philip no longer has any say in the running of his family. There are many scenes of the redecoration of Clarence House under his direction. He wants the family to stay there. He insists that the Queen puts this proposal to Churchill. It is understood that, in real life, the Queen and Prince Philip would have preferred to stay at Clarence House, which was the perfect London home for a young family, not too big, and with a well-sized garden. Buckingham Palace has always served multiple purposes: a series of state rooms, offices for members of the Household, and the King's and Queen's rooms along a long corridor on the Constitution Hill side. It must have been a bit like living in an Edwardian hotel. But Churchill insisted that the monarch must live in the Palace, and so they moved in on 5 May 1952. The Queen Mother stayed on, only moving into Clarence House on 18 May 1953.

The other issue is the family name. This was another genuine cause for Prince Philip to be upset. In this episode, Lord Mountbatten, curiously dressed for dinner as an Admiral in his own home (Broadlands), boasts, with some justification, that the House of Mountbatten now reigns in Britain. Normally the male who marries a Queen Regnant gives his name to the new house; hence Queen Victoria was the last Queen of the House of Hanover, which became Saxe-Coburg when she married Prince Albert in 1840. Prince Ernst August of Hanover was at Mountbatten's table in 1952 and did not like what he heard. He informed Queen Mary, who called for Jock Colville, then Private Secretary to Winston Churchill. The Prime Minister duly informed the Queen that the Royal House must be called the House of Windsor. There is a fictional scene in which the Queen reads out this declaration to the Privy Council.

It is true that Prince Philip was livid about this, though in reality he wanted it called the House of Edinburgh, rather than Mountbatten, the preferred choice of his ever-manipulative uncle. Harold Macmillan record-ed that Prince Philip wrote a well-reasoned memorandum making his case, but the Government would not countenance the Mountbatten name being used. In opposing Prince Philip, ministers such as Macmillan were keen to send 'a shot across his bows', to keep the young consort in his place.

The Duke of Windsor comes over for his brother's funeral, and the series makes much of the newly-styled Queen Mother's hostility to him. The Duke of Windsor also wants various things. There is a lot of bargaining in this episode. The Queen asks Churchill to do her a favour by informing the Cabinet about the Mountbatten name, claiming that she is keeping him in office by agreeing to a delayed Coronation. In fact the Coronation was always planned for June 1953, as it takes a long time to arrange such a ceremony.

Then Churchill asks the Duke of Windsor to be an intermediary with the Queen for the other two issues of this episode: the family name and the move to Buckingham Palace. In exchange, the Duke wants to retain the allowance King George VI promised him (which ceased at the King's death), and again demands an HRH for the Duchess. There is a curious scene in which three contrasting aspects of love are explored: we see a sequence with the Windsors dancing romantically, the Queen and Prince Philip at the opera (where he takes her hand), and Princess Margaret popping into Townsend's office to kiss him with some passion.

The Duke of Windsor then lunches with the Queen, which did not happen in real life, and puts Churchill's two points to her. Most erroneously, we find the young new Queen turning to the Duke of Windsor for avuncular advice. He is presented as a sage, and explains, in the almost Shakespearian language the scriptwriters give him, why she, as a monarch, must move from Clarence House to Buckingham Palace.

Alex Jennings, the actor, looks incredibly like the Duke of Windsor, but the real life Duke never delivered such Shakespearian oratory. Nor would the real Queen ever have asked for advice from a man so patently incapable of giving it.

The Duke of Windsor had been immensely tiresome ever since the Abdication in 1936, and Tommy Lascelles had seen him off on more than one occasion, most effectively in 1945. The Royal Family felt gravely let down by the Abdication, and Lascelles wrote at one point in the 1940s that any appearance in Britain by the Duke would have a grave effect on the health and peace of mind of George VI. Later on, in real life, the Queen was considerate to her uncle, and various rapprochements were made before he died. But the trouble with the Duke of Windsor was that if he was given an inch, he would take a mile.

In other themes, we see Prince Philip asking Group Captain Townsend to teach him to fly, a theme followed up in the next episode. He did learn at White Waltham, near Maidenhead, but was taught by Flight Lieutenant C.R. Gordon, of Cheltenham. He received his wings from Air Chief Marshal Sir William Dickson, on 4 May 1953, having flown for 90 to 100 hours.

The film-makers also introduce the idea that Prince Philip bullied Prince Charles, which is again addressed in later episodes.

Minor mistakes: Prince Philip was a descendant of the royal houses of Greece and Denmark, but not of Norway. King Haakon of Norway (1872-1957) was a Prince of Denmark who was given the Norwegian throne in 1905.

A recurring mistake throughout the series: all the characters arrive at Buckingham Palace through the ceremonial front gates. Normally they enter via the gate to the right near Constitution Hill.

Episode 4—Act of God

This is a curious episode based on the great fog that descended on London between 5 and 9 December 1952. This fog encouraged some spontaneous burglaries and one murder. London was perfectly used to fogs, so it was not treated as a particular emergency until much later, when it was estimated that between 4,000 and 12,000 people died – though most of them had breathing problems or were very old. Most of this episode is fantastical and did not happen. Obviously the scenes involving Churchill's fictional secretary, Venetia Scott, were made up. She is killed when hit by a bus due to the fog. Since there was no public transport working, other than trains on the London Underground, this could not have happened.

The film-makers then introduce Churchill failing to take action; the question of Clement Attlee, the Leader of the Opposition, potentially turning the situation to political advantage; and Churchill's decision to visit a hospital during the crisis. All this is fiction too. Interestingly, the fog did not rate a mention in Martin Gilbert's official biography of Churchill.

The other scenes involve Prince Philip learning to fly and Government annoyance at this. Queen Mary falls ill and takes to her bed, attended by Sir John Weir. The Queen walks through the fog to visit her ailing grandmother to discuss what is expected of her as a monarch.

Episode 5—Smoking Mirrors

There is a flashback to 11 May, with George VI explaining the significance of anointing in the Coronation ceremony, and talking of the weight of the crown, both actual and symbolic. The action then moves forward to 1953, with the Queen trying on the same crown before her Coronation.

Queen Mary falls gravely ill, which brings the Duke of Windsor over. In this series he comes from France, though he actually came with his sister, the Princess Royal, from New York. There are lots of opportunities for him to complain to the Duchess of Windsor about his family, his mother, and his treatment. The Queen is warned by the Queen Mother to be wary of the Duke: 'Like mercury, he'll slip through the tiniest crack.' During his visit, the Duke is summoned from Marlborough House to Lambeth Palace, where he finds the Archbishop of Canterbury, Tommy Lascelles, and one other, ranged against him explaining why he should not attend the Coronation and why the Duchess would not be invited. The Duke is furious, but he agrees to put out a statement explaining why he won't be there.

While he is at Lambeth Palace, a message comes through that Queen Mary has died. In reality the Duke was not at Lambeth Palace. Her funeral is shown (with the Royal Standard on her coffin, not her personal standard).

In real life, the question of the Duke's possible attendance at the Coronation preoccupied the Archbishop of Canterbury as early as November 1952, and he raised the matter with the Queen at lunch. It was agreed that his presence 'would create a very difficult situation for everybody, and if he had not the wits to see that for himself, then he ought to be told it.' Churchill took the line that while it was understandable that the Duke would wish to be present at family funerals, it would be completely inappropriate for him to attend the Coronation of one of his successors. Tommy Lascelles wrote to the Duke's lawyers, making it clear that no summons would be forthcoming. A statement was prepared for the Duke to issue to save face, but he must have alarmed the British Government by giving an interview at Cherbourg in which he said he might well be in England at the time of the ceremony. As it happened, he and the Duchess stayed in Paris and watched it on television with friends, a scene recreated in this episode. We see the Duke explaining the proceedings in the Abbey, again in Shakespearian phrases, to a group of undistinguished guests. The episode ends with him playing his bagpipes outside the house, with tears in his eyes, presumably to hint that he is regretting all that he discarded.

The other main theme in this episode is the role of Prince Philip in the preparations, and also in respect of the part he intends to play in the ceremony. Here he only agrees to chair the Coronation Committee if he has total control, and we see him coming out with all sorts of modern ideas for the day, such as inviting Trade Union leaders and businessmen to take part. He is told that some things cannot be changed. There is a row with the Queen and he tells her he refuses to kneel before her to do homage. In the end he is obliged to do so, but he is given credit for insisting the ceremony be televised.

Having written a book on the Coronation and delved into the Archbishop of Canterbury's papers, I can testify that these reveal the Archbishop of Canterbury pushing Prince Philip out as much as possible. He pronounced: 'There must be no association of him in any way with the process & rite of Coronation.' Yet they also show that Prince Philip was quite happy to do fealty after the Archbishop (when he could have been expected to go first), and that he presented a silver gilt wafer box to the Abbey, and a chalice and paten to Lambeth, as a form of offering to respect taking his place next to the Queen during the communion.

Unlike other flaky consorts, such as Prince Claus of the Netherlands and Prince Henrik of Denmark, Prince Philip was raised within the Royal House of Greece. But for the birth of the future King Constantine in 1940, he would have ended up as King of Greece in 1964, and marriage with Princess Elizabeth would have been out of the question. In real life he adapted quickly to his changed circumstances, but in *The Crown*, they put him in conflict at every opportunity.

The Coronation was a wonderful opportunity to create a scene of great visual magnificence, but it fell seriously short in regard to a great number of details. Earl Mountbatten, seated in the front row of the Royal Box (he was not in the front row) appears dressed in ducal robes, and is not wearing his Garter collar. Nor is the supporting actor representing the Queen's uncle, the Duke of Gloucester. The Marquess of Salisbury carries the Sword of State (which he did at the actual Coronation), but he crowns himself with an Earl's coronet. The Dowager Duchess of Devonshire (Mistress of the Robes) fails to put on a coronet. The oath was not administered during the anointing, but before it. There are a number of Peeresses sitting where the Peers sat in reality. Thus this important scene proves disappointing.

The St Edward's Crown with which the Queen is crowned is far too big, but this may have been intentional, to demonstrate the burden the Queen was assuming.

Episode 6—Gelignite

The theme of this episode is the Princess Margaret/Peter Townsend love affair and their attempt to marry in 1953. The opening scene shows the Queen and Prince Philip going to the Coronation Derby, but we then see a newspaper office where an unshaven journalist has picked up what he realises is a huge scoop (hence 'gelignite'): Princess Margaret having been observed picking some fluff off the jacket of Group Captain Peter Townsend at the Coronation – he being by then a divorced equerry. Princess Margaret and Townsend are on the point of accompanying the Queen Mother on an official visit to Rhodesia.

The Princess invites the Queen and Prince Philip to dine with her and Townsend, and they believe that they have her blessing, but they soon run up against the establishment. Tommy Lascelles invokes the Royal Marriages Act of 1772, which stated that no lineal descendant of George II could marry without the consent of the Sovereign, and so Princess Margaret is asked to wait for two years. The series suggests that the Queen deceived her sister by appearing to support her wish to marry him and then eventually forbidding it. The film-makers imply that the Princess never forgave her sister, a theme which recurs in later episodes. The sequence of events is somewhat muddled. Since there are also a number of contradictory accounts left by Peter Townsend, Tommy Lascelles, and Princess Margaret to her biographer, it is hard to settle on a true version, since that true version depends on which source is trusted.

Lascelles appears at his most severe in this episode, a Satanic and menacing figure. This is an interpretation that might well have resonated with the real life Princess Margaret, not to mention the real life Peter Townsend.

There is no doubt that Princess Margaret fell in love with the Group Captain. He was the trusted equerry of the father she adored and a Battle of Britain hero. He was rather a gentle figure. However, as Lascelles made clear to him in no uncertain terms, he had been placed in a position of trust and responsibility. He was a married man with two sons and he was considerably older than the Princess. The real Lascelles said of him: 'He has Theudas trouble,' a reference to the *Acts of the Apostles*: 'For before these days rose up Theudas, boasting himself to be somebody.' Churchill made it clear that the Queen could not sanction the marriage. So Townsend was sent away to Brussels, where he stayed for two years. By the time he returned in 1955, when the British public were agog to know whether the marriage would take place, the path of love had completely run its course. This is the main theme of Episode 10.

Minor mistakes: The costume department gave Townsend his CVO, but failed to give the actor playing Lascelles any medals or Orders (by 1953 he was entitled to a GCVO, CMG, MC and various other medals); in Rhodesia, there was a Governor-type figure in a Guards tunic with a GCB, but only bar ribbons for medals. At one point we see the telephone switchboard, which includes Highgrove House. This is the house that the Duchy of Cornwall bought for Prince Charles in 1980, so it would not have been on the switchboard in the 1950s.

Episode 7—*Scientia Potentia Est*

It is 1940 and the Princesses are with their French governess. Princess Elizabeth goes to Eton College to be instructed by the Provost, Sir Henry Marten (not Vice-Provost as stated in the series). This leads to the Queen wishing to be better educated – knowledge is power – and as the story moves on into 1953, one of the themes is that she wants a tutor to help expand her general knowledge. Martin Charteris arranges such a figure called Professor Hodge, but he is a completely fictitious character. The Queen did not seek a tutor to help her, and nor would she ever have taken advice on constitutional matters from a figure outside the Palace system.

Retirement, or rather non-retirement, is in the air. Churchill is getting old and rather desperate, but refusing to go. The Anthony Eden character is ill in Boston – rather luridly so. He is taking injections, the implication being that he was almost a drug addict (a theme which gets worse in subsequent episodes). Then Churchill has two strokes. Evidently the Queen is not informed, and so the fictitious Hodge urges her to summon Churchill and Lord Salisbury to tick them off like recalcitrant schoolboys. *The Crown* plays out the two wiggings. Symbolically this is to demonstrate that the Queen is getting on top of her role as an assured constitutional monarch.

Tommy Lascelles is also about to retire. In this series, the Queen wants her former Private Secretary, Martin Charteris, to take over, and even offers him the job. He and his wife (Gay in real life, but here carelessly called Mary – the name of his daughter) go to look at the Private Secretary's new home at St James's Palace and have a tree trimmed outside it. They even say the house will be good for 'the girls'. (In real life they had the one daughter and two sons). Michael Adeane hears about this, is aggrieved, and complains to Lascelles, who engineers that Adeane succeeds him and not Charteris. Once again Lascelles proves himself more dominant and the Queen's private wishes are set aside.

This is inaccurate. It is traditional that the monarch's serving Private Secretary stays on for a few months at the beginning of a new reign to help with the transition, as did Lascelles until after the Coronation, retiring at the age of sixty-six on the last day of 1953. Michael Adeane and Martin Charteris were working as a team (along with Edward Ford, who is not portrayed in the series). Michael Adeane was always the natural successor, and there was no fuss. He took over.

In this episode, the film-makers have put a 1972 story into a 1953 context, presumably so that they could use the Lascelles figure. There was a fuss over Adeane's successor when he retired. At that time Charteris was the natural successor, but Lord Cobbold, a former Governor of the Bank of England, wanted to sweep away the Guards Officer Old Etonian types who held sway in the Palace, and replace them with more meritocratic types. He tried to reject Charteris in favour of Philip Moore. But Charteris went to see the Queen and asked to take over. She immediately agreed, and he proved to be an inspired Private Secretary, who succeeded perhaps better than any other Private Secretary in presenting her to the world as she really is. He served until 1977.

The message that emerges from this episode is that the Queen is conscientious, prepared to do her homework and research, with a knack for discovering the truth when it is kept from her – as, for example, with Churchill's two strokes (though Lord Salisbury is unlikely to have been wilfully withholding this information from her).

Lascelles is well played in the series, though his older daughter (now ninety-four) has said that his hair parting is wrong and his moustache too big. By curious misfortune, the actor playing Michael Adeane looks more like the real life Martin Charteris.

Episode 8—Pride and Joy

The King used to say of his two daughters: 'Lilibet is my pride, and Margaret my joy.' (This is something first published in my biography of the Queen Mother, and therefore explains the title of this episode.) Here there is a complete jumble of the real life facts. The episode starts with a scene where the Queen unveils a statue to King George VI in the Mall. This was in fact unveiled on 6 October 1955. But suddenly plans are being made for the Commonwealth tour of 1953 and 1954, so the story moves back in time.

There is particular discussion about Gibraltar as a place that could be dangerous. This was quite true. There were threats from the Spanish, and for a visit of less than two days, there were detectives from Scotland Yard operating under cover there for several months. There are some scenes from the Commonwealth tour demonstrating the Queen's determination to undertake it all, and the strain this put on her. At one point the press see the Queen and Prince Philip emerging from a house after a row. Rightly, they stress the success of the tour.

The film-makers decided that while the Queen was away on her Commonwealth tour, the country would be run by Princess Margaret, rather than the Queen Mother. They use her as a modernizer, breaking all the rules and introducing a spontaneous and touchy-feely (quasi-Diana, Princess of Wales) approach to being Head of State which, not surprisingly, upsets everyone. She rewrites a speech, suiting her wayward personality and introducing more colour into it, and delivers this at an Ambassadors' reception (curiously, British Ambassadors serving overseas, in Washington and Athens, who appear to have flown in for this party). She gets the guests laughing. The point they seek to make is that Princess Margaret thinks she would make a better Queen than her sister, more in tune with the changing times. The Charteris figure gets more and more worried as she chats to miners, gives spontaneous interviews to the media in which she mentions her affection for Townsend, and takes a dig at the Queen. She gets ticked off by Churchill, who begins to detect a crisis arising, akin to the Abdication. When the Queen comes back, Churchill alerts her to Princess Margaret's behaviour.

None of the above happened and is ultimately tabloid invention. Nor do I subscribe to the idea that there was bitter jealousy between Princess Margaret and the Queen. Princess Margaret always supported her sister.

To achieve this, they blur the dates. They have the Queen Mother out of the way, buying Barrogill Castle (later renamed the Castle of Mey) in Scotland, something which actually happened a whole year earlier, in 1952. Lascelles (who would by then have retired) tells the Queen Mother what her duties will be, but she tells him she wants to be away. The episode twists history by suggesting the Queen Mother was prepared to shirk all her responsibilities.

In reality the Queen Mother was very much in London while the Queen was away, not least looking after Prince Charles and Princess Anne, who stayed with her at Royal Lodge most weekends (when she was not away racing), and at Sandringham for a long Christmas holiday. She was the senior Counsellor of State during the Queen's absence. Counsellors act in tandem and Princess Margaret usually assisted her. Churchill had the same kind of audiences with the Queen Mother as he would have done with the Queen, but not so regularly. The series also has Princess Margaret being advised by Martin Charteris, when in real life, he was travelling with the Queen and Prince Philip.

As to the Castle of Mey scenes, the Queen Mother did not ride horses after the early 1930s, so to see her cantering along the beaches is somewhat strange. Nor is it likely that the castle's funny old owner, Captain Imbert-Terry, would not have recognised her. While she stays with the Vyners, she addresses the issues of her early widowhood. As this is meant to be late 1953, and not 1952, this does not convince – even with dramatic licence.

Minor mistakes: at a fitting they dress Prince Philip in the naval uniform which he wore but once – at the Coronation – an outdated uniform with epaulettes; later, he wears a Garter riband and bar medals, which is incorrect. The Caribbean Governor in white is wearing what might be a curious interpretation of a military GBE riband along with a huge GCMG star. When Princess Margaret gives her speech, the guests are wearing Orders, but she is not.

Episode 9—Assassins

In London in 1954, Jean Wallop, a private person still very much alive, arrives in a restaurant to dine with Lord Porchester (later 7th Earl of Carnarvon). He proposes to her. She accepts on one condition – that he does not still hold a torch for 'her' – i.e. the Queen. I have it on impeccable authority that the future Lady Carnarvon did not even realise that he knew the Queen when she met him. The outcome of this scene is that he tells her that for the Queen there was only ever Prince Philip, and she (his bride to be) is the only one for him. The Porchesters were married in January 1956.

The Crown suggests that Porchester was the man many wanted the Queen to marry, and they hint that she would have been happier with him than with Prince Philip. For the record, the Queen Mother originally wanted Princess Elizabeth to marry a Grenadier Guards officer. The late Duke of Grafton springs to mind. But from very early on, she set her heart on the good-looking Prince Philip. In 1947 they were engaged. The Queen Mother told Sir Arthur Penn, 'Won't the Grenadier Guards be disappointed?' They were, and at first refused to have Prince Philip as their Colonel.

The episode depicts Porchester ringing the Queen late at night, with a certain number of *double entendres*, his wife-to-be coming through from the bathroom. The Queen's love of racing is emphasized, as is Prince Philip's boredom with it. This theme is rather dropped as the episode goes on, though in one scene, the Queen and Prince Philip watch a mare being covered, with Lord Porchester observing from afar and giving some predictably cheap lines. Afterwards Prince Philip jumps out of the Land Rover in a rage. This is followed by a scene back home, with a declaration of love by the Queen for Prince Philip.

Lord Carnarvon was a close adviser to the Queen, as her racing manager, and she often stayed with him and his wife to visit studs in the Berkshire area. Both she and Prince Philip flew down from Balmoral to attend his funeral in 2001.

The Graham Sutherland story is well-told. Sutherland was commissioned to paint Churchill's portrait, to be presented to him in Westminster Hall for his eightieth birthday on 30 November 1954. Peter Morgan is on firm ground here, as it is within the political domain. Intermingled with this is the theme that Churchill should stand down. There is a fictional scene where Eden visits Churchill at Chartwell, and bids him to give way in a histrionic, hysterical manner – presaging the recurring theme that he was some kind of junkie. As to the portrait itself, it was revealed after her death in 1977 that Lady Churchill had destroyed it. In 1957 she described Churchill's reaction to the painting in a letter to Lord Beaverbrook: 'It wounded him deeply that this brilliant…painter with whom he had made friends while sitting for him should see him as a gross & cruel monster.'

There is a partly fictitious version of the speech he gave in Westminster Hall, in which he teases the audience that he is about to retire and that his successor, Anthony Eden, is to hand. It appears that he then promptly re-signs, and with the brutality of the political system, as he leaves the Palace, Eden's car draws up. The Queen's speech at Churchill's farewell dinner was taken from a private letter from the Queen to Churchill after his resig-nation and not delivered as such on the night. As we listen to it, we see another scene: Lady Churchill presiding over the burning of the Sutherland portrait.

In reality Churchill did not resign immediately after his birthday in November 1954. He hung on in office until April 1955.

Episode 10—Gloriana

The episode reprises the events of December 1936. Edward VIII agrees to see his brother, the Duke of York, but not the Duchess (there is no evidence for that). Then the new King informs his daughters that their uncle has put love before duty. He tells them never to let each other down, thus introducing the theme that there could be tension between them later on.

A Royal Standard is hoisted over Balmoral. It is Princess Margaret's twen-ty-fifth birthday (21 August 1955), and she declares she still feels the same way about Group Captain Townsend. It seems possible that she can now marry him. But the Queen discusses the Royal Marriages Act with Michael Adeane. He invokes a different version of the situation. He mentions that both Houses of Parliament need to be informed and that if they object, she would need to wait for twelve months. Still under the illusion that she is free to marry, Princess Margaret wants to announce it.

Another scene shows Prince Philip teaching Prince Charles to fish, so that we realise that he is quite tough on the boy. The Queen Mother voices the opinion that Prince Philip is taking it out on Charles due to the frustrations of his own life. *The Crown* likes to think that the Queen Mother was very thick with Lascelles in his retirement. She relied on him a bit after the King's death but Lascelles took a dim view of her philosophy of life, considering it was best summed up in the hymn: 'the rich man in his castle, the poor man at his gate' But it gives them the idea that Prince Philip was sent by the Queen to open the Olympic Games in Melbourne, Australia in November 1956 to get him out of the way: away from bullying his son and in the hope, as expressed clearly in this episode, that he would come back 'changed'. But this all happens in August 1955 and he did not undertake the voyage until October 1956.

The second and final round in the Princess Margaret/Peter Townsend drama is played out. We see headlines speculating as to whether or not she is going to marry the Group Captain. Apparently Prince Philip is somewhat in league with Princess Margaret over the marriage question. Townsend returns and they run together in a passionate embrace. Then come the problems, the involvement of the Attorney-General, the threat that Lord Salisbury will resign if the marriage takes place, the Queen saying she will support her in any way she can, but then that she would be deprived of money and titles, and have to live abroad for several years as Mrs Peter Townsend. Princess Margaret claims the country is on her side. The invented words of their father about mutual support are repeated by the Queen.

Then it all gets worse, with the Cabinet advising against the marriage, the Archbishop of Canterbury and other Bishops reminding the Queen that she is Defender of the Faith and of the oath made at the Coronation, and finally the Queen seeking advice from the Duke of Windsor in France.

He tells her 'You must protect the kingdom'. And so, in this episode, the Queen's line is that Princess Margaret cannot marry Townsend and remain part of the family.

In reality, Eden did advise the Queen at Balmoral, but there was no involvement from the Archbishop, and the Duke of Windsor was in no position to pontificate about the roles of sister or Queen, or of duty to the realm.

The film-makers maintain that Princess Margaret broke off from Townsend because she had been forbidden to marry him. Furthermore, she tells him she will never marry anyone else. And then Townsend makes a public statement, in fact reading much of the written statement that in reality Princess Margaret issued to the press. He then returns to Brussels.

In truth, the decision was a mutual one between Princess Margaret and the Group Captain, largely based on the fact that Lascelles's separation plan had worked and the love between them had died.

None of the characters are happy at the end of this episode. Princess Margaret is seen depressed at parties, and Peter Townsend sitting forlornly alone in his apartment in Brussels. Prince Philip is angry at being sent away on the long tour.

The situation with Nasser in Egypt is flagged up during this episode. We see meetings with Eden, more pills being taken, and in the end, Anthony Eden slumped in front of burning cine-film of Nasser, having just stuck a needle full of drugs into his arm. This is followed by an image of the Queen posing in tiara and evening dress next to the Crown Jewels, which have been brought to the Palace for effect. She is shown as an assured and confident young monarch, while the ever-frustrated Prince Philip drives off down the Mall in his open car, all alone, looking distinctly fed up.

I should be grateful that it is Cecil Beaton who gets the last word in both this series and Series 2, extolling the virtues of monarchy with Shakespearian lines. Nevertheless, Claire Foy's Queen looks ominously sad.

Viewers then had to wait a year to find out why.

SERIES TWO

Episode 1—Misadventure

Series 2 opens with a scene implying that the marriage of the Queen and Prince Philip was so desperate that they would have liked to divorce. There is much talk of Prince Philip playing second fiddle, complaining, whingeing, and whining, and the Queen feeling humiliated. This scene comes after the voyage in *Britannia* in October 1956, when he went to open the Olympic Games in Melbourne and then toured the South Atlantic. It then flashes back to scenes before the trip, and includes a contrived moment when the Queen puts a cine camera into his briefcase and discovers a photograph of a ballerina. Pre-publicity for *The Crown* suggested that this ballerina was a creation of fiction, but, most improbably, the series named her as Galina Ulanova, the feisty *prima ballerina assoluta* of the Bolshoi Ballet, very much a real person.

Young television viewers will not have heard of Ulanova, but she was immensely famous. Her 1956 visit with the Bolshoi was the cultural event of the season, almost as exciting at the time as Nureyev's arrival in 1962. David Webster, Director of Covent Garden, described her and her visit as 'a miracle.' The Bolshoi came to London after nine years of negotiations, and Margot Fonteyn and the Sadler's Wells Ballet went to dance in Moscow. She was more proficient and distinguished than beautiful. The ballet dancer Antoinette Sibley described her: 'She was a mess. She looked like an old lady...this old woman got up from the stalls. We thought she was the ballet mistress.' Born in 1910, Ulanova was then 46 years old, and it is impossible that Prince Philip could have met her, as she had never been to England before. Her only contact with Britain was an English teddy bear her mother had bought her when she was two. Ulanova arrived in Britain on 1 October, and Prince Philip came down from Sandringham on 9 October and left for his trip on 15 October. Ulanova was accompanied on this trip at all times by her husband.

The Queen Mother took Prince Charles to a matinée. Princess Margaret went and so did the Edens. The Queen attended alone on 25 October, when Ulanova chose to dance *Gisèle* for her, as it was the role in which she was most proficient.

Later in the episode Princess Margaret refers disparagingly to the Thursday Club, and goes so far as to suggest that an osteopath (clearly Dr Stephen Ward – see episode 10) procured ballerinas and others for the members. Ulanova was one of the ballet's most successful stars, and the suggestion (vague as it is) that such a distinguished, not to say matronly, ballet dancer might have been a Stephen Ward protégée is completely wide of the mark.

The other theme of the episode is the Suez crisis: Anthony Eden, his potentially duplicitous role in the crisis, Nasser, the Israeli involvement, Mountbatten advising the Queen, Anthony Nutting giving words of warning, and secret deals with the French. Here Peter Morgan is on stronger ground, as he has Robert Lacey as his historical adviser, and Lacey spoke to Lord Mountbatten when researching his book, *Majesty* (1977). In the Hartley Library in Southampton is a letter from Lacey to Mountbatten, assuring him that there is no danger of him being identified as the source about Eden and Suez for his book. What Mountbatten told him was that the Queen disapproved of Eden's policy, and when Eden (by then Lord Avon) read this in serialisation he threatened to sue Lacey. Martin Charteris stepped in to soothe ruffled feathers. Maybe the Queen did know, but Mountbatten did not always tell the truth, particularly to authors.

Then the episode portrays Princess Margaret, still drunk the morning after another late night partying, and still blaming the Queen for her unhappiness on account of the Peter Townsend debacle from Series 1. There are gratuitous reminders of the infidelity of Edwina Mountbatten with Nehru. And the theme is introduced that Eileen Parker is unhappy about the prolonged absence from family life of her husband, Mike Parker, who is travelling with Prince Philip. That was indeed the case.

Episode 2—A Company of Men

This episode concentrates on Prince Philip's voyage in *Britannia* between October 1956 and February 1957, more or less ignoring the official stopovers and making it appear that he hated formality and was only happy playing games such as cricket and tug-of-war. There are scenes with him dancing and watching bare-breasted girls dancing. There is a grainy image of a man descending onto one of these women for sex – hard to see, but probably the Mike Parker character. There is a scene in which a Tongan man is rescued, and Prince Philip has *Britannia* turned round to take him home: a chance for more bright-eyed local girls to lure him to dance. There is no evidence for this. A journalist called Helen King is invented to interview the Prince in Australia, and he clearly accepts the invitation to talk to her in order to seduce her. She annoys him with her questions and he storms out, but the implication is clear. At one point the trip is summed up as 'a five-month stag night – whores in every port.'

An incriminating message is read out by Baron to the Thursday Club amidst raucous laughter. We see Eileen Parker getting hold of a girl who works at the club, and asking for evidence against her husband, Mike. The girl hands over the letter. The Queen is even seen calling unexpectedly on Mrs Parker at her home, only to be told in no uncertain terms that she, Mrs Parker, has sacrificed enough for the Royal Family. She goes to her lawyer and starts the process of separation leading to divorce. There was no visit by the Queen to Mrs Parker.

In 1982 Eileen Parker wrote a book called *Step Aside for Royalty*, a frank account of her experiences, aiming to set the record straight. This makes it clear that her main resentment was that her husband was away too much with Prince Philip, missing family anniversaries, and generally finding his life as a Private Secretary more interesting than being with her. She hints at Parker's infidelity, but she certainly did not obtain any evidence of this in 1956. Furthermore, there can have been no letter for Baron to read out to the raucous company of the Thursday Club, not least because Baron (Stirling Henry Nahum) had died on 5 September 1956, and Prince Philip and Mike Parker did not set off for their trip until 15 October.

In his posthumously published memoirs, Baron took credit for founding the Thursday Club after the war. He wrote: 'I suggested forming a little club to lighten the gloom that surrounded us all, and that we should meet with friends once a week. No issues of importance would be allowed, no international questions would be solved. The club would be devoted to absolute Inconsequence. We would eat as well as we could, tell stories and swop reminiscences…The lunches lasted well into the afternoon, spreading consternation and dismay through our liver-systems and playing havoc with afternoon appointments.' Mrs Parker described it as 'a luncheon club organised by Prince Philip and Mike for entertaining kindred spirits'. She continued: 'They would meet for long meandering lunches at Wheeler's in Soho and entertain themselves during the meal with speeches, pranks and jokes.' Mrs Parker wrote that the Queen referred to the members as 'Philip's funny friends.' That is all she wrote about the Thursday Club.

This episode also contains two Christmas speeches, one by Prince Philip from *Britannia* and one from the Queen at Sandringham. These cryptic messages are exchanged over the air waves, the Prince Philip character saying: 'We are men together, but we each stand alone.' Arguably the speeches devised for *The Crown* were warmer and more human, even better, in fact, than those actually delivered. The real life Prince Philip said: 'We are absent, most of us, because there is a Commonwealth…I hope all of you at Sandringham are enjoying a very happy Christmas and I hope you children are having a lot of fun. I am sorry I am not with you.' He ended on a religious theme: 'We pray, in words used thousands of years ago, that the Lord watch between me and thee when we are absent from each other.'

The real Queen sent a greeting to him and all serving on *Britannia*: 'If my husband cannot be at home on Christmas Day, I could not wish for a better reason than that he should be travelling in other parts of the Commonwealth…On his voyage back to England, he will call at some of the least accessible parts of the world, those islands of the South Atlantic separated from us by immense stretches of the ocean, yet linked to us with bonds of brotherhood and trust.'

The rest of this episode is involved with the Suez crisis, with Eden relying more heavily on pentobarbitane pills. There are suggestions that the Queen's two private secretaries, Michael Adeane and Martin Charteris, acted as spies on the Queen's behalf.

Minor mistake: as an Admiral of the Fleet Prince Philip would be entitled to fly the Union Flag, rather than a White Ensign, on *Britannia.*

Episode 3—Lisbon

The first issue is the return of the Prime Minister, Anthony Eden, from a recuperative break in Jamaica. He thinks he can resume office, but Harold Macmillan turns on him. 'There's no justice in politics,' Macmillan tells him. Eden realises the game is up and resigns. The Queen reiterates an earlier theme, by suggesting that Eden wanted to make a name for himself by going to war in Suez – emerging, as it were, from Churchill's shadow. She also makes it clear to Macmillan, when he becomes Prime Minister, that she is aware that previously he had supported the war. Despite a bit of dramatic license here, it is generally accepted that Macmillan turned on Eden, and certainly Eden's wife never forgave him.

There is more espionage in the Private Secretary's office, Tommy Lascelles being brought into play to manage the Parker crisis. In this episode, it is suggested that Mrs Parker is suing for divorce, at which point, on board *Britannia*, an angry Prince Philip informs Mike Parker: 'You know the rules,' and demands his instant resignation. Parker leaves *Britannia* in Gibraltar.

In reality Eileen Parker sought a separation, rather than a divorce. According to her book, she did not intend this to become public knowledge while her husband was at sea with Prince Philip, but her lawyer, Meryn Lewis, put out a statement without consulting her – he gave a scoop to Rex North of the *Sunday Pictorial*. As a result, Parker's marriage came to an end and so did his career as a royal courtier, something which Mrs Parker maintained she had not intended to happen. In her book, Eileen Parker wrote: 'I learned that both Prince Philip and the Queen had tried to dissuade Mike from resigning.' But his solicitor stated: 'With all the worry in the present circumstances of his marriage he feels he cannot give of his best.'

His courtier life did not end immediately. He stayed on with Prince Philip for some months, was invested with a CVO by the Queen in March, and was in attendance when Prince Philip attended the wedding of his niece, Princess Margarita, in Baden in June 1957. When Mrs Parker finally sued for divorce in 1958, she cited a certain Mrs Thompson for adultery (in July 1957). Following the divorce, Eileen immediately married a man called Tom Prentice, who worked for Stanley Rous at the Football Association, which may partly explain her wish to move on. Parker himself did not remarry until 1962.

There is no evidence of Lascelles being involved in any of this. But in real life an announcement was given to the press a week after Parker's resignation on 5 February – therefore on 12 February: 'It is quite untrue that there is any rift between the Queen and the Duke.'

Their marriage has now lasted over seventy years.

Towards the end of the episode, the imagined show-down between the Queen and Prince Philip is repeated. It ends with him demanding to be given new status. And there is a Camelot-style scene where he is invested with a sword of state, a ring, and a sceptre, crowned with a ducal coronet (such as he had worn at the Coronation four years earlier), with what looks suspiciously like a Baron's robe draped over him. As we know, he was already a Duke.

Prince Philip has never been interested in titles, least of all for himself. The main reason to create him a Prince of the United Kingdom was that George VI had forgotten to do so, when he created him HRH and Duke of Edinburgh in 1947. Lord Mountbatten wanted it and so did Prince Philip's aunt, Queen Louise of Sweden, who was disappointed that he had turned it down in 1955. Mountbatten wrote to her in 1957: 'Lilibet has got the new Prime Minister – in consultation with Commonwealth colleagues – to ask for Philip to be made "The Prince" on return from this tour, & we all hope he'll agree this time.' The honour was given to recognise his service to the Commonwealth on the long voyage. To portray him as demanding the status is wrong.

The Crown's conclusion is that the marriage continued in quest of the survival of the monarchy. Peter Morgan considers that one of their principal interests is their own survival. There is an alternative view – that they devote their lives to the service of the nation and Commonwealth. The Queen has also played a significant role as a conciliator internationally, particularly with countries such as Germany, Japan, Russia and China, and, more recently in the public memory, with Ireland.

Minor errors: Sir Michael Adeane retained his moustache in real life; Cecil Beaton never photographed Prince Philip (other than at the Coronation); the *Britannia* trip lasted four months, not five.

Episode 4—Beryl

Colin Tennant weds Lady Anne Coke at St Withburga's, Holkham, on 21 April 1956. Princess Margaret is there with the Queen Mother (they both were), and present with his camera is the young Antony Armstrong-Jones. By now miserable after having lost Townsend, she agrees half-heartedly to marry Billy Wallace, a member of the Margaret set. This goes wrong later when Wallace (depicted as a coward) fights a duel with Colin Tennant and is wounded. There was no such duel in real life. But in the episode, Princess Margaret ditches Wallace, and afterwards we see her staggering around in her bedroom, whisky in hand, looking completely demented.

Later, Cecil Beaton (poorly dressed compared to the real Cecil) comes to photograph her, and is given some prosaic lines about his approach to the fantasy of beauty as he poses her. The results are stunning but she does not like them. Enter Lady Elizabeth Cavendish, her 'new' Lady-in-Waiting (in fact appointed in October 1954), who invites her to a dinner where she meets Tony again. He flirts with her and persuades her to be photographed. There follow meandering scenes in his studio, where he subtly disconcerts her and makes her fall in love with him. Another bedroom scene shows her back home, much happier, clearly in love. Tony takes her photo, with naked shoulders – the one shown was actually taken ten years later in 1967, after their marriage in 1960. They ride about on motorbikes, and yes, they did do that.

It is true that Lady Elizabeth Cavendish introduced Princess Margaret to her more Bohemian friends in the hope of amusing her. She produced Tony Armstrong-Jones, but she, like many others, was greatly surprised when they married, as that had not been part of the plan.

There is a further scene in which the new Prime Minister, Harold Macmillan, talks of the importance of good relations with the Americans, telling the Queen of the importance of sustaining a good 'marriage' in international politics. This gives the film-makers the chance to point out the problems in his own marriage. His wife, Lady Dorothy, has been pursuing a long affair with the politician, Bob Boothby, and they drop in the canard that her daughter Sarah (later Heath, who died in 1970) might have been Boothby's love-child.

Macmillan was tortured for forty-five years by the suspicion that Sarah was Boothby's child. When Sarah was born in 1930, Dorothy told him that Boothby was the father in order to get him to leave her. This would have ruined his political career. The marriage survived. In 1975, nine years after Dorothy's death in 1966, and five years after Sarah's tragic death following a brain haemorrhage, Macmillan ran into Boothby at Julian Amery's house in Eaton Square. He asked for a private meeting with Boothby, who assured him that Sarah was a Macmillan. As D.R. Thorpe put it in his biography *Supermac*: 'Boothby was a rakish figure, but in one thing he was very careful. Despite – or perhaps because of – having so many affairs, he ensured he never left behind what the Victorians would have called "a vestige".'

Episode 5—Marionettes

This episode ends with a real life photograph of John Grigg, the former Lord Altrincham, and professes that Buckingham Palace maintained that he had done more to help the monarchy than any other figure in the twentieth century. In this episode we have an accurate portrayal of Altrincham's attack on the Queen, how he was slapped across the face by a member of the League of Empire Loyalists, and how his words caused a major re-think within the Palace walls.

The true course of events was that Malcolm Muggeridge had written about 'The Royal Soap Opera' in *The New Statesman* in October 1955. This caused minimal stir, but Altrincham's article in *The National and Evening Review* in August 1957 turned him into an arch-villain overnight, causing Muggeridge's piece to be reprinted with a similar effect. Altrincham received 2,000 letters of complaint, was anathematized by the Archbishop of Canterbury, menaced with many threats and, yes, he was slapped by an elderly member of the League of Empire Loyalists.

Altrincham was far from anti-monarchist, but he saw the need for change. He attacked the Queen's education and the monarchy's way of life: 'the London season, racing, the grouse moor, Canasta and the occasional royal tour.' He lambasted presentation parties at which debutantes paraded in front of the Queen as a 'grotesque survival from the past'. He saw the monarchy as being able to fire the popular imagination, 'not just as a symbol of stability and continuity, but as a positive force for good in the world.' This led directly to a number of changes – the abolition of presentation parties, appointments to the Royal Household from different walks of life, the informal luncheon parties, and so on.

This episode introduces the fantasy that the Queen made a dire speech at a Jaguar factory, written by Michael Adeane with the approval of Lascelles. The Queen and Duke did visit the Jaguar factory near Coventry on the same day that she laid the foundation stone for the new cathedral – 23 March 1956. But there is no evidence of a speech, nor is there evidence of the Queen engineering a face-to-face meeting with Altrincham to discuss his article. Nor would the first guests coming to an informal luncheon have come along in morning coats and garden party hats.

Episode 6—*Vergangenheit*

Vergangenheit means 'the past', so Episode 6 kicks off with dramatic scenes (and thriller music, as for a John Le Carré adaptation) as a captured German officer shows where he buried a vital tin box containing the Marburg Papers, which were deemed to contain material proving that the Duke of Windsor had been a traitor to his country during the Second World War.

The episode introduces the Queen's interest in the evangelist, the Rev Billy Graham. He represents the spirit of forgiveness, which is concerning the Queen in respect of the Duke of Windsor. She invites Graham to preach and afterwards they talk. As the episode progresses, the Queen asks him about forgiveness, since she has been considering forgiving her uncle.

The episode employs a device to create conflict. It tells a version of the Marburg Papers saga. It then depicts the Duke of Windsor asking the Queen to sanction him to get a job. As would be expected, every possible accusation is aired against the Duke – particularly in a scene when the Queen asks Tommy Lascelles to spill it all out, which he does: Mrs Simpson having an affair with Ribbentrop, Hess wanting to reinstate the Duke as King, the Duke visiting concentration camps on his 1937 visit to Germany, holding the Duke personally responsible for the German occupation of Paris, and so on. At the end of the programme, to back up their point, they show some real photos of the Duke on his German visit, to convince the viewer that all this happened.

So where is the truth in any of this? The Marburg Papers did exist and extracts were published from time to time, causing the Duke of Windsor considerable annoyance in the 1950s and 1960s. When the first batch was published by the Americans in 1954, Churchill told the Duke that they were harmless and had been put in 'to add some sensationalism to what would otherwise be a very boring book.' More came out later, but to little avail. As Philip Ziegler, the Duke's official biographer, put it: 'Many other fantasies have been voiced in the last thirty years. The laws of libel mercifully ensured that the most grotesque have only been published after his [the Duke's] death.'

Then there is the question of the Duke's quest for a job. On his return from the Bahamas in 1945 the Duke did try to get a job, and he also re-peated his request that the Duchess be made an HRH and received by the King and Queen. He was put firmly in his place by Tommy Lascelles, who asked him not to continually plead for these things. The Duke wriggled a bit, but in effect he did go away. Presently he settled at the house in the Bois (here called the Villa Windsor, a name it was only given years later by Fayed), and also bought his Mill outside Paris. There were never any plots to make him Ambassador in Paris, or a roving Commissioner for the Commonwealth.

This episode has a fantasy that the Duke was not allowed to come to Britain without the Sovereign's permission. This is untrue, and he came whenever he pleased, but obviously informally. The Windsors stayed with the Earl of Dudley, they went to see *Oliver!* on stage, etc., and in 1965 he spent some time in the London Clinic for an eye operation, when the Queen visited him twice. In June 1967 the Duke got his longed-for meeting with the Royal Family, when both appeared for the unveiling of the memorial to Queen Mary in the wall of Marlborough House. By an agreement made in 1961, the Queen permitted them both to be buried at Frogmore. He died in 1972 and she in 1986.

There was no question of the Queen sending him away as a traitor, as she does towards the end of this episode. The vilification of the Duke is completed with the Prince Philip character congratulating the Queen for 'banishing Satan from entering the Garden of Eden.' The Duke of Windsor may have been a fool, but he was no traitor.

Episode 7—Matrimonium

The scene is Brussels in August 1959, and Group Captain Peter Townsend is preparing to marry a nineteen-year-old girl called Marie-Luce Jamagne. This episode concerns the somewhat unconventional courtship of Princess Margaret and Tony Armstrong-Jones, and is full of quasi-erotic scenes – Tony with Jacqui Chan, Tony with Princess Margaret, and Tony lying on a bed with Camilla Fry, along with his first choice of best man, her husband, Jeremy Fry. Obviously there is a lot of dramatic licence here, since no-one knows what goes on behind closed doors in bedrooms (or in photographic studios, for that matter). We are treated to a bare-breasted Camilla Fry, the buttocks of her husband, Jeremy, as he joins her and a naked Tony on the bed, and a fair amount of sexual activity in the studio, not only with Jacqui Chan but also with Princess Margaret. One scene with Jacqui Chan is heralded with Tony sporting an erection concealed within his white trousers.

It is hard to keep up with Tony Armstrong-Jones's amatory exploits, but we now know a lot more following Anne de Courcy's 2008 biography of him. In the series, the Queen gives a lavish party and gets suspicious about Mrs Fry. She asks Michael Adeane to investigate, and he turns to Tommy Lascelles to help form the case against Armstrong-Jones. They inform the Queen about Jacqui Chan, Robin Banks, Gina Ward, and both Mr and Mrs Jeremy Fry.

In real life Tony had had an affair with the actress Jacqui Chan, but that was over by 1960. She was invited to his wedding. Robin Banks was a one-time long-suffering assistant. She did not have an affair with him, as she was in love with someone else. Georgina Ward, a lovely actress, did have an affair with him, but most complicated of all was his relationship with the Frys.

It was revealed many years later that Tony was the father of Camilla Fry's daughter, Polly, who was born on 28 May 1960, three weeks after his wedding. For the record, Jeremy Fry was asked to step down as Tony's best man. His place was taken by Dr Roger Gilliat. This was due to a homosexual conviction – 'importuning for immoral purposes'. Fry was from the Quaker chocolate family. In 1955 he had married Camilla Grinling. They had two sons and two daughters before divorcing in 1967. Camilla died in 2000, and Jeremy in 2005.

It demonstrates a certain amount of chutzpah on the part of Armstrong-Jones that he went to the altar of Westminster Abbey to marry the Queen's sister when, if he gave it a thought, he might have realised that he had just begat a child on his best friend's wife. Fortunately, Princess Margaret never knew about the paternity of Mrs Fry's daughter.

There are two points which make something of a nonsense of this episode. The first is the conceit that Tony only married Princess Margaret to gain the approval of his mother, Anne, Countess of Rosse. It is evidently true that Tony thought his mother did not respect him. Her character is played by a good actress, Anna Chancellor, except that in real life Lady Rosse was much too practised a performer on the social scene ever to portray what she was really thinking. She lived in a dream-like world of her own imagination, lying in bed in the mornings writing long handwritten letters to friends, and conjuring descriptions of her brother, Oliver Messel, as 'Darling Angel Oliver'. In real life she was somewhat more than pleased about the marriage to Princess Margaret. She herself had risen from being Anne Messel to Countess of Rosse, and society called her 'Tugboat Annie' on the grounds that she 'drifted from peer to peer.'

Another conceit is that Princess Margaret was determined to marry before Townsend. He got engaged in October 1959 and married Marie-Luce on 21 December. Princess Margaret did not get engaged until February 1960, and the film-makers have invented some dodgy protocol that the engagement could not be made public until Prince Andrew was born, since they decide that no announcement can be made 'until the Sovereign's child is born.' It is true, however, that the Queen asked for the announcement to come after Prince Andrew's birth. But it seems that Tony and Princess Margaret agreed to marry somewhat after Townsend's announcement of his engagement.

Episode 8—Dear Mrs Kennedy

Here is a chance to see the workings of the Commonwealth. The episode opens with President Nkrumah in full voice in Accra, declaring that Ghana is a free country, and that they are all Africans. The Queen's picture is taken down, and one of Lenin is put up in its place. Part of the issue is where Ghana will side – with the Russians or with the Americans, and whether it will stay in the Commonwealth.

Two other themes are brought into play here. One is the Queen observing an old oak on the Balmoral estate, that has passed its best and must be felled – a filmic symbol of the decline of British influence in Africa. Then there is the visit of President John F. Kennedy and his wife, Jackie, to Paris. The Queen feels middle-aged, and the film-makers suggest that she felt insecure about Jackie Kennedy, jealous of her and threatened by her.

In the episode, the Kennedys are coming over to Britain, and the Queen and Prince Philip invite them to dine at Buckingham Palace. Many of the male guests want to sit next to Jackie, but Prince Philip insists he should (which is of course correct etiquette). According to the episode, he flirts with Jackie. The Queen shows her round the Palace and is rather taken by her, but then discovers that Mrs Kennedy has made disparaging remarks, and presently the Queen prises these out of her friend and equerry, Lord Plunket. He tells her that Mrs Kennedy thought the Palace run-down, the institution of monarchy out-dated, and the Queen herself middle-aged, incurious, unintelligent and unremarkable.

It is apparently this that inspires the Queen to go out to Ghana and win Nkrumah round by dancing the foxtrot with him. She returns in triumph. The film-makers hit the message on the head by having JFK congratulate his wife on influencing the course of foreign policy – in that without the jibes the Queen would not have gone – and then there is an invented scene in which Mrs Kennedy comes to Windsor Castle to apologise and explain her ill-advised comments.

We then fast forward to see the oak being felled in the park. It is now November 1963 and the Queen and Prince Philip witness the events surrounding President Kennedy's assassination. The Queen breaks protocol by asking that the tenor bell at Westminster Abbey be sounded, something which only happens on the death of a member of the Royal Family or a Dean of Westminster. (The bell was duly sounded for an hour on Saturday 23 November).

Now we must examine the facts, since what they have done in this episode is to take two independent events, both of which did happen (the dinner for the Kennedys on 5 June 1961 and the visit to Ghana between 9 and 20 November 1961), and clash them together to create a drama, throwing in the old oak tree for symbolic reasons.

The Queen entertained the Kennedys to dinner on 5 June. The President and his wife were coming to Britain for a private family christening for Jackie's niece, Christina Radziwill. Though it was not required that the Queen should entertain them, she offered to do so. There was a dinner party at Buckingham Palace and some question as to whether Stas and Lee Radziwill (Lee being Jackie's sister) should be invited, since both had been divorced. In the end the rule against inviting divorced people was relaxed, though a few days later the Queen's aunt, the Duchess of Gloucester, complained to her sister-in-law, the Duchess of Buccleuch, that the Queen had been forced to entertain 'some people called Radziwill' as if things were getting seriously out of hand.

There exist two sources for Jackie's disparaging comments. One is Gore Vidal's 1995 memoir, *Palimpsest*, in which he dug into some notes made in 1961 and added some afterthoughts. From other things written by Vidal, I suspect he may have subscribed to the Noël Coward philosophy of never letting the truth get in the way of a good story, but let's take him at face value. Evidently Jackie Kennedy told Vidal that the Queen had refused to invite either Princess Margaret or Princess Marina (both of whom the Kennedys wanted to see), but had produced a number of Commonwealth agriculture ministers. She found the Queen 'pretty heavy-going'. Gore Vidal added that he had repeated this to Princess Margaret years later, who said: 'But that's what she's there for.'

Here is Vidal's paragraph in full, the italics representing what he wrote in 1961:

'*I think the queen resented me. Philip was nice, but nervous. One felt absolutely no relationship between them. The queen was human only once.'* Jackie had been telling me about the Kennedy state visit to Canada and the rigors of being on view at all hours. ('I greeted Jack every day with a tear-stained face.') *The queen looked rather conspiratorial and said, 'One gets crafty after a while and learns how to save oneself.' Then she said, 'You like pictures.' And she marched Jackie down a long gallery, stopping at a Van Dyk to say, 'That's a good horse.'*

So, no flirting.

The night afterwards Jackie told Cecil Beaton, 'They were all tremendously kind and nice, but she was not impressed by the flowers, or the furnishings of the apartments at Buckingham Palace, or by the Queen's dark-blue tulle dress and shoulder straps, or her flat hair.'

The idea that Mrs Kennedy returned for a further meeting in order to explain herself to the Queen, as in the episode, is fabrication.

The Queen's proposed visit to Ghana was certainly a complicated issue. Nkrumah had been Prime Minister since 1952 and President since Ghana became a Republic in March 1957. He was becoming increasingly despotic. There were distinct fears that Ghana might leave the Commonwealth, as South Africa had done, as recently as 31 May 1961. There was a suggestion that the Russians might finance the Volta Dam project.

The Queen had been meant to go to Ghana earlier, but became pregnant with Prince Andrew, so had to cancel. She did not want to disappoint Nkrumah. Meanwhile he had visited Russia in October, the political climate was turbulent, two bombs had gone off in Accra, and there were genuine fears for the Queen's safety. Duncan Sandys, then Secretary of State for Commonwealth Relations, was sent out to test the water. All went well, and the Queen remained determined to go. Macmillan wrote of her: 'She loves her duty and means to be a Queen and not a puppet.' She told him, 'How silly I should look if I was scared to visit Ghana and then Khruschev went and had a good reception.' So she went, and as shown in the episode, melted Nkrumah by dancing with him at the state ball. After the visit

Macmillan was able to telephone President Kennedy and tell him: 'I risked my Queen. You must risk your money.' As a result, the Americans financed the building of the Volta Dam, and Ghana stayed in the Commonwealth. This had nothing to do with upstaging Mrs Kennedy.

Episode 9—Paterfamilias

This centres around Prince Charles at Gordonstoun, so there are lots of muddy boots, bullying, freezing, wet dormitories, cold showers and exacting cross country runs. We know that Prince Charles hated his time at Gordonstoun, and most people conclude he would have been happier at Eton, where, in the fullness of time, he sent his own sons. So that is the first theme exploited with full (and acceptable) dramatic licence. Amusingly, however, Kurt Hahn, Prince Philip's headmaster, is still running Gordonstoun in 1961 – he would have been seventy-five years old by then. In reality he retired in 1953.

The clashing theme is Prince Philip at Gordonstoun. He was sent there in the 1930s after prep school at Cheam and a brief spell at school at Salem. Kurt Hahn moved to Gordonstoun to avoid Nazi Germany, and Prince Philip joined him there. Being a more robust figure than his eldest son, he thrived at the school, acquitted himself well, and there is an argument that it made him the self-reliant man he is today.

This episode introduces a further drama, which perverts the facts. We see the young Prince Philip flying in a plane with his sister, Princess Cécile of Hesse, and we are told she is a nervous flyer. Then Prince Philip gets into a scrape at school, punches a boy, and so, instead of having him in Darmstadt for half-term, Cécile flies to England (the implication being that, but for this apocryphal incident, she would not have flown) while heavily pregnant. The plane crashes and she is killed. Prince Philip attends the funeral – much is made of the Nazi atmosphere in Darmstadt (true), though he himself is a contrasting figure to the uniformed Nazis, in his black overcoat. At the reception afterwards, his be-monocled father, Prince Andrew of Greece, shouts at him, 'It's true, isn't it, boy? You're the reason we're all here burying my favourite child.'

The facts are as follows. Cécile and her family did fly to Britain, and they were all killed when the plane hit a factory chimney in fog near Ostend on 16 November 1937. But the reason they came was a long-planned commitment to attend the wedding of Cécile's brother-in-law, Prince Ludwig of Hesse, to Hon Margaret Geddes. When I was working on an authorised biography of Prince Philip's mother, one of the first things his archivist, the late Dame Anne Griffiths, told me was that one of the great sadnesses of Prince Philip's life was the death of his sister, made worse by the knowledge that she was pregnant. The baby was in fact born during the flight as a result of the trauma associated with the crash.

The implication of this episode is that Prince Philip as good as killed his sister, which as the above facts show, is untrue.

The point the episode wants to make is that Prince Philip was ill-treated by his father, and then did not hesitate to submit his son to the same unpleasant school life. When the fictional Prince Charles is upset and wimpy in the aeroplane, Prince Philip shouts at him that he is 'bloody wet'. When they arrive back at Windsor, Prince Philip runs off to play with Princess Anne, and Prince Charles is led forlornly into the castle.

Minor mistakes: Lord Mountbatten writes on crested paper, but the coat of arms is that of the Marlboroughs not the Mountbattens; Windsor Castle scenes were filmed at Belvoir Castle – usually with the Royal Standard hanging in the hall, but in one scene they failed to change it, and instead we see the Garter banner of one of the Dukes of Rutland.

Episode 10—Mystery Man

The first scene shows Prince Philip waking with a cricked neck, made worse by his subsequent exercises outdoors. He is sent off to see the osteopath, Stephen Ward, who sorts him out, and then explains that the Prince is probably tense and that he could maybe help him. He invites him to one of his notorious parties, and there is mention of Christine Keeler and Mandy Rice-Davies. 'My neck's feeling better already,' says the Prince, seizing another opportunity for potential lascivious behaviour. It is not explicit that he does go, but he is soon heading off for weekends away and travel overseas, even when the Queen is pregnant with Prince Edward (informed of this good news by that homeopathic quack, Sir John Weir, one of five doctors who signed the bulletin when the new Prince was born).

Moving on a year, John Profumo is in trouble, and is summoned for a chat over a game of billiards with Harold Macmillan, on his return from an afternoon on the grouse moors. Macmillan tells his wife that years in politics have taught him when a man is lying. She calls him 'a credulous, trusting fool'.

This is the swinging sixties. Lady Dorothy attends a performance of *Beyond the Fringe*, and persuades Macmillan to go along too. As ever, Peter Morgan is much more convincing when he is treating politics than the Royal Family. The Profumo/Stephen Ward drama is played out: the questioning of Christine Keeler, the arrest of Stephen Ward, and presently his trial and suicide. All this is fine.

Macmillan's resignation and the appointment of the Earl of Home as his successor is another theme. It is suggested that at first the Queen refused to accept Macmillan's resignation over the Profumo affair. What actually happened was that Macmillan wrote to the Queen in June 1963 apologising for the 'development of recent affairs', without offering to resign. He decided to step down in October following a prostate operation, realising that it was time to go. By citing ill-health he avoided being pushed out by dissidents in his party following the Profumo scandal.

There was a lot of political scheming behind the scenes, but Macmillan realised that the Palace wanted one name to be recommended as the next Prime Minister, not seven. So he prepared a memorandum which concluded that the Earl of Home should be sent for. He asked the Queen to visit him in hospital and gave her this advice (on 18 October) while he was still technically in office, and so she was constitutionally required to take it. While Macmillan may have been anxious to kill Rab Butler's chances of taking over, he was also keen not to put the Queen in a difficult position.

The Queen received Home later the same day and invited him to form an administration. The late Ben Pimlott described the Queen's acceptance of Home over Butler as 'the biggest political misjudgement of her reign', but Macmillan's biographer, D.R. Thorpe refuted this, not least since Butler's chances with the party were slim.

The possible involvement of Prince Philip and Stephen Ward is hinted at with no evidence to support it. In June 1963, at the height of the scandal, there were what Richard Davenport-Hines has called 'outrageous headlines for non-existent stories.' The *Daily Mirror* printed one: 'PRINCE PHILIP AND THE PROFUMO SCANDAL – RUMOUR UTTERLY UNFOUNDED.' The paragraphs that followed failed to specify any such imagined rumour.

Stephen Ward sketched numerous public figures, some better than others. He was given commissions by the *Illustrated London News* and the *Daily Telegraph*. His sitters included Princess Margaret, the Queen's uncle, the Duke of Gloucester, her aunt, the Princess Royal, and figures such as Archbishop Makarios, Nancy Astor and Sir John Rothenstein. He sketched Prince Philip. Amongst his more outré portraits is a naked Mandy Rice-Davies, reclining as if posing for a Lucian Freud portrait. Today Ward's pictures fetch thousands of pounds in the saleroom, but no one is suggesting that the late Duke of Gloucester or the late Princess Royal were frolicking in Lord Astor's swimming pool at Cliveden.

The episode heads towards its end, and the finale of the series, with the Queen confronting Prince Philip with the photograph of Ulanova from Episode 1. He sidesteps this, but asserts that he is ultimately the one person who is forever completely loyal to her. This would appear to be a sop from the film-makers, a curious back-tracking after spending a considerable part of twenty episodes painting him in dismal light.

Another minor mistake: Princess Marina complains of the noise as Princess Margaret's workmen modernise her apartment at Kensington Palace. She tells the Queen that this noise is even annoying the Gloucesters. 'Everything irritates the Gloucesters,' says the fictional Queen. It must have been very noisy, since the Gloucesters did not live at Kensington Palace then. They were some miles away in York House, St James's Palace.

ABOUT THE AUTHOR

HUGO VICKERS is a writer, lecturer and broadcaster, an acknowledged expert on the Royal Family and a frequent commentator on radio, television and in newspapers. He has written biographies of many twentieth century figures, including the Queen Mother, Gladys, Duchess of Marlborough, Cecil Beaton, Vivien Leigh, Princess Andrew of Greece and the Duchess of Windsor. His book *The Kiss* won the 1996 Stern Silver Pen Award for Non-Fiction.

He is also Chairman of the Outdoor Trust (which puts walkways into Commonwealth countries and overseas territories), a Deputy Lieutenant for the Royal County of Berkshire and Captain of the Lay Stewards of St. George's Chapel, Windsor.

He worked as an historical adviser to films *The King's Speech* and *Victoria & Abdul*.

He lives between London, Wiltshire and Windsor, and has three teenagers, Arthur, Alice and George.

Printed by Printforce, United Kingdom